TSUNAMIS

MICHAEL WOODS AND MARY B WOODS

LERNER BOOKS • LONDON • NEW YORK • MINNEAPOLIS

To Jeremy Woods

Editor's note: Determining the exact death toll following disasters is often difficult – if not impossible – especially in the case of disasters that took place long ago. The authors and the editors in this series have used their best judgement in determining which figures to include.

First published in the United Kingdom in 2008 by
Lerner Books,
Dalton House,
60 Windsor Avenue,
London SW19 2RR

Website address: www.lernerbooks.co.uk

This edition was updated and edited for UK publication by Discovery Books Ltd.,
Unit 3, 37 Watling Street, Leintwardine, Shropshire SY7 0LW

British Library Cataloguing in Publication Data

Woods, Michael, 1943-
 Tsunamis. - (Disasters up close)
 1. Tsunamis - Juvenile literature 2. Tsunami damage -
 Juvenile literature
 I. Title II. Woods, Mary B.
 363.3'494

 ISBN-13: 978 1 58013 457 6

Printed in China.

Contents

Introduction

ON 26 DECEMBER 2004, THE WATER SUDDENLY PULLED AWAY FROM THE BEACH IN PHUKET, A CITY IN THE SOUTH-EAST ASIAN COUNTRY OF THAILAND. IT WAS ONLY 9 AM, BUT PEOPLE WERE ALREADY OUT ENJOYING THE SUN. MOST WERE TOURISTS HAPPY TO ESCAPE THE COLD WINTER WEATHER BACK HOME. THIS PART OF THE WORLD IS A FAMOUS HOLIDAY SPOT.

Many people were curious. They walked out to explore the seabed. It had been under water just seconds ago. How cool! They saw fish flopping, seashells and rocks. Children waded into holes in the seabed and splashed away.

This video still captured a tsunami wave hitting the coast of Malaysia in 2004.

Other tourists, napping on blankets, ignored it all. In hotels and shops along the beach, workers also went about their business. They didn't even notice.

Then they saw a wall of water. 'You saw a blue-black dark wall spring to life,' said Rick Von Feldt, who was on the beach. 'You could tell the water was coming back.'

MONSTER WAVE

The wall of water, at least 10 metres high, was a monster wave – a tsunami. An earthquake under the Indian Ocean started the tsunami. The wave travelled through the water for 4,800 kilometres (3,000 miles) before slamming onto coasts across southern Asia and eastern Africa. 'Suddenly this huge wave came, rushing down the beach, destroying everything in its wake,' said Simon Clark, a photographer. 'People that were snorkelling were dragged along the coral and washed up on the beach, and people that were sunbathing got washed into the sea.'

One wave followed another. 'The second wave carried a car right towards me,' said Les Boardman, 'but I was able to shift to one side and watch it shoot past. The worst part was, you could see the bodies going out in the water.'

DEATH AND DESTRUCTION

Boree Carlsson rushed into a hotel as the waves rolled in. 'As I was standing there, a car actually floated into the lobby and overturned,' he recalled.

The great Indian Ocean tsunami swept people out to sea, where they drowned. It picked others up like dolls and threw them against the ground. The waves were strong enough to pick up fishing boats and drop them in the middle of streets. Buses and cars swirled through the water.

One entire town of 30,000 people disappeared after the waves crashed through. Homes, schools and shops were flattened like sand castles hit by a normal sized wave. The tsunami killed about 200,000 people. Another 43,000 others are missing and presumed dead.

A satellite image showed the flooding and devastation on Phuket Island, Thailand, after the 2004 Indian Ocean tsunami.

What Is a Tsunami?

TSUNAMIS ARE WAVES THAT CRASH DOWN ONTO THE SHORE AND CAUSE DISASTERS. DISASTERS ARE EVENTS THAT CAUSE GREAT DESTRUCTION. SOME TSUNAMIS ARE MORE THAN 30 M HIGH. TSUNAMIS CAN BE HUNDREDS OF KILOMETRES LONG. THEY CAN TRAVEL THOUSANDS OF KILOMETRES AT SPEEDS OF NEARLY 950 KILOMETRES PER HOUR. THAT'S AS FAST AS JET AEROPLANES FLY.

The word *tsunami* comes from the Japanese words *tsu* (harbour) and *nami* (wave). Unlike regular waves, tsunamis do not stay on the beach or in a harbour. They rush inland. They can sweep up people and destroy buildings.

ONE AFTER ANOTHER

Tsunamis are not just one wave. They are several waves that line up in a row. They wash onto the land one after another. Have you ever been knocked down by a wave at the beach? Imagine the effects of a monster wave with enough water to flood hundreds of football pitches.

Though the wave below is large, it is not nearly as large or powerful as most tsunami waves.

Nicaragua's Masachapa Beach is littered with the debris of wrecked homes and boats following a massive tsunami in 1992.

One tsunami in 1908 was so powerful that it destroyed almost all of Messina, Italy, then a city of 150,000 people. The tsunami also wrecked the nearby city of Reggio di Calabria. Waves up to 12 m high washed over the coasts. As many as 200,000 people may have died in that tsunami. It was the worst ever tsunami in Europe.

Tsunamis kill and injure people by sweeping them up. The waves then bash people against the ground, trees or buildings. Stones, splinters of wood, and sand in the waves also hurt people. Many people drown when the tsunami washes them out to sea.

DISASTER WITHOUT WARNING

Unlike hurricanes, blizzards and many other disasters, tsunamis often occur with little or no warning. That's especially true for local tsunamis.

Tsunamis cause different amounts of damage. They can drive planks of wood through tyres (above) and destroy bridges and flatten villages (left).

Most of Messina, Italy, was reduced to rubble after the 1908 tsunami.

Local tsunamis are waves that strike land near the place where they formed. In a local tsunami, waves could come onto the shore just fifteen or twenty minutes after they first rise up in the ocean.

Sonam Kalra and her husband were taking a walk on the beach the day of the Indian Ocean tsunami. 'Suddenly we heard someone telling us to run,' she said. 'We saw a big wave coming towards us.' Water soon surged over the couple's heads. They had to cling to a pillar to stop themselves drowning.

Tsunami waves move through great expanses of ocean water without being noticed. Then they rise up near the shore and roar onto the land. That makes tsunamis especially dangerous. People often don't have time to take cover before tsunamis strike. As a result, tsunamis can be very deadly.

Collapsed buildings at the pier on Thailand's Ton Sai Bay in December 2004

Fishing boats washed into town in Kodiak, Alaska, USA during a 1963 tsunami.

'*Mayday, Mayday* – Erdie *in Lituya Bay* . . .
I think we've had it – *goodby[e]!*'

– *Howard Uhlrich, radioing a Mayday message (a call for help)
from his boat, the Erdie, in Alaska during a 1958 tsunami*

27 August 1883
KRAKATAU

An artist captured the devastating 1883 Krakatau eruption in this drawing.

In August of 1883, the Krakatau volcano exploded. This volcano is on an island in the South-east Asian country of Indonesia. Krakatau's explosion may have been the loudest sound that humans ever heard. People heard it 4,800 km (3,000 miles) away.

The explosion dumped two-thirds of the island into the ocean. Imagine the waves that a person makes by diving into water. Then imagine the waves when most of an island splashed in!

'At seven in the morning we suddenly saw a wall of water was coming closer to our ship. . . .' wrote a passenger on the steamship *Gouverneur Generaal Loudon*. The ship, anchored near the town of Teluk Betung, almost sank. **'Not long after**

Tsunamis often carry large items inland. This steamship was carried away by the Krakatau tsunami.

there were still three other such tremendous waves...everything leapt on the beach right before our very eyes. We saw the lighthouse was broken like [a] match stick and houses disappeared, crushed by the waves.'

The waves rolled into almost three hundred other towns along the shore. People had no warning that the waves were coming. The first hit about an hour after Krakatau blew its top.

One wave was 40 m high. That's as high as the windows on the thirteenth floor of a skyscraper. The waves picked up one warship in the harbour and dropped it about 2.5 km (1.5 miles) inland. When people returned to their villages, they found chunks of rock from the ocean floor. The rocks weighed more than 450,000 kilograms.

Eustatius Pechler tried to outrun the tsunami, but it caught up with him. He woke up in the dark, battered and bruised. Pechler headed back home to the town of Merak. On the way, he saw a train engine. It was 300 m away from the track. Nothing was left in the town. Everything had been washed out to sea – people, animals and buildings.

The tsunami killed about thirty-six thousand people. For weeks after the disaster, sailors in ships found the bodies of victims floating in the ocean. The tsunami injured thousands. About 165 towns were destroyed and 132 were damaged.

'Teluk Betung was just [a] sea of water.'

– unnamed passenger on the steamship Gouverneur Generaal Loudon, describing the 1883 tsunami that swept through Teluk Betung, Indonesia

What Causes Tsunamis?

REGULAR OCEAN WAVES HAPPEN WHEN WIND BLOWS OVER THE TOP OF THE WATER. THE WIND HEAPS THE WATER UP INTO PEAKS THAT ROLL OVER THE SURFACE. TSUNAMIS ARE DIFFERENT FROM REGULAR OCEAN WAVES. IN A TSUNAMI, SOMETHING GIVES THE WATER A SHOVE. THEN THE WHOLE OCEAN MOVES — FROM TOP TO BOTTOM.

What can cause the ocean to move? Undersea earthquakes can shake up the waters. Volcanic eruptions and landslides can cause ocean movement too. When a disturbance happens, waves spread out from the area of the disturbance. The waves travel quickly. They move far across the sea. When the waves reach shallow water near the coast, they rear up into monster waves. They become tsunamis.

TSUNAMI VS TIDAL WAVE

Many people call tsunamis tidal waves. That's a mistake. Tsunamis have nothing to do with tides. Tides are the daily rising and falling of the ocean water. A tsunami may look like a fast ocean tide rushing onto the shore or away from it. Tides do not cause tsunamis, but Earth movements and volcanic eruptions do.

GIVING THE OCEAN A SHOVE

Earthquakes that happen under the ocean are the number one cause of tsunamis. Since 1945 more people have died from tsunamis caused by earthquakes than from ground-shaking earthquakes themselves. It usually takes an earthquake with a strength of at least 7.5 on the Richter scale (a scale for measuring earthquakes) to produce a destructive tsunami. The Indian Ocean tsunami was caused by one of the strongest quakes ever recorded on Earth. It was at least 9.0 on the Richter scale.

HOW A TSUNAMI FORMS

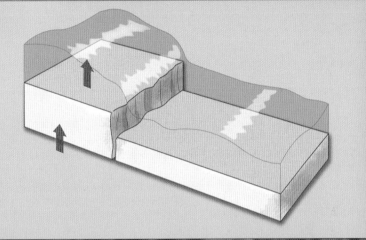

A disturbance – such as an undersea earthquake – disrupts the water.

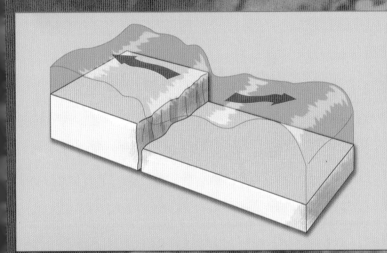

Waves spread out from the area of the disturbance.

The waves reach shallow coastal waters and lose speed. Then they grow large and race towards shore as a tsunami.

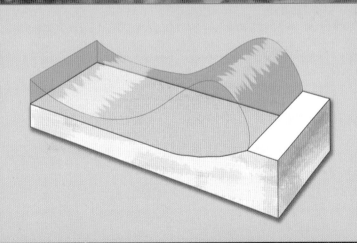

The earthquake cracked an area of the Indian Ocean floor about 400 km (250 miles) long and 95 km (60 miles) wide. One big part of the seabed thrust up about 3 m. That sudden movement gave the water a shove, much like a giant's hand sweeping under the surface of a swimming pool. It set about 114 trillion litres of water into motion. That's nearly enough water to cover the entire country of Spain to a depth of almost 30 centimetres. The water moved out in a shock wave in all directions from the centre of the earthquake.

LANDSLIDE TSUNAMIS

Undersea landslides can also cause tsunamis by pushing water outwards. There are many mountains on the ocean floor. Landslides happen when rocks and soil suddenly tumble down the mountainside. When the rock falls, the water around it gets pushed out of the way.

Earthquakes cause some landslides. A 1998 tsunami that killed thousands of people in Papua New Guinea happened when an earthquake caused a landslide under the Pacific Ocean.

Landslides above the ground can also cause tsunamis. A landslide made the largest tsunami ever seen on Earth. It happened in July of 1958, when 40 million cubic m of rocks splashed into Lituya Bay, Alaska. An earthquake shook the rocks loose. Their splash made a wave 525 m high.

People often drown in tsunamis. After the 1998 Papua New Guinea tsunami, villagers buried the dead where they found them. They covered them in driftwood *(right)* or buried the bodies in the sand.

A 1983 tsunami in Japan brought widespread flooding. An earthquake that measured 7.7 on the Richter scale caused the tsunami.

VOLCANO TSUNAMIS

Volcanoes erupting below the ocean or on the ground are another cause of tsunamis. Explosions occur when some volcanoes erupt. Volcanic explosions under the sea can push water outwards or trigger undersea landslides that cause tsunamis. Explosions on the Earth's surface can blow volcanoes apart and dump huge amounts of rock and ash into the ocean.

One of the worst tsunamis in history happened when the Krakatau volcano exploded in Indonesia in 1883. The waves destroyed towns and villages on the islands of Java and Sumatra.

TSUNAMIS FROM OUTER SPACE

As far as we know, another kind of tsunami has happened only in disaster movies. This kind of tsunami could happen if a comet or asteroid from outer space smashed into the Earth. Comets are big chunks of ice and dust. Asteroids are chunks of rock. A comet or asteroid that splashed into the ocean could cause huge waves.

Scientists say an asteroid just 5 km wide could cause a terrible disaster. If such an asteroid crashed into the middle of the Atlantic Ocean, it could cause a tsunami large enough to drown cities all along the East Coast of the United States and flood huge sections of western Europe.

LUCKY BABY 81

The 2004 Indian Ocean tsunami carried many people out to sea. The waves dropped other people in safe places. A child known as Baby 81 *(below)* was among the lucky ones. He wound up in a rubbish pile in Sri Lanka. Nobody knew his name. Hospital workers called him Baby 81 because he was the eighty-first patient that day. Nine different couples thought Baby 81 was their child. It took two months and DNA tests to identify the real parents – Murugupillai Jeyarajah and his wife, Junita. Baby 81 – whose real name is Abilash – finally went home with his mother and father.

This Japanese woodblock print is from the 1800s. It shows an 1855 earthquake that caused a large tsunami and fires that destroyed almost 15,000 Tokyo homes.

An aerial view of Chile's coast shows damage from the 1960 tsunami. Many residents died from the tsunami waves. They could not escape the earthquake in their small boats.

22 May, 1960
CHILE

People thought the worst was over when the ground stopped shaking. It was 22 May 1960. The strongest earthquake ever recorded had just happened off the coast of Chile, South America. The earthquake was close to the shore. It caused a tsunami. The waves travelled only a short distance before hitting land. People did not have time to escape. Within ten to fifteen minutes, tsunami waves up to 23 m high roared into cities and villages along the nearby coast. The tsunami killed up to two thousand people in Chile and neighbouring Peru.

The tsunami and earthquake also smashed the homes of two million people. They caused damage estimated at £265 million. That was just the start of one of the worst tsunami disasters in history. The tsunami raced across the Pacific Ocean. Within fifteen hours, it had travelled 9,656 km (6,000 miles) to Hawaii.

Susan Maeda Veriato was an eyewitness in the Hawaiian city of

Waves from the Chilean tsunami destroyed part of Hilo, Hawaii.

'

Suddenly I heard a shout,
'Big wave!'

'

– *Susan Maeda Veriato, on the*
1960 tsunami in Hilo, Hawaii

Hilo. '*The streetlights around us*
exploded,' she said.

James Fujimoto was in bed when he heard a sound like a jet plane outside the window. '*I looked out of my window, and saw sparks flying and a huge wave, around 20 feet [6 m high], coming towards our house,*' he said. '*Then my family awoke. We all moved into the living room*

when the wave hit. . . . *We all grabbed each other and before we knew it, our neighbours' houses came smashing into ours like a sandwich, we being in the middle. We spun around 2 [to] 3 times. . . . As water seeped inside, I could feel our house sinking.*'

The waves killed more than sixty people in Hawaii. It caused damage estimated at £12 million. Soon the tsunami reached California, USA. In Crescent City, waves may have reached 4 m. They destroyed fishing boats and caused other damage.

After a journey of twenty-two hours and 16,100 km (10,000 miles), waves 3 m high reached Japan. There they killed about 120 people, destroyed or flooded thousands of houses and sank hundreds of ships.

From higher ground, residents of Onagawa, Japan, watch a Chilean tsunami wave pour into their town.

Tsunami Country

TSUNAMIS CAN HAPPEN IN OCEANS AND OTHER LARGE BODIES OF WATER ALMOST ANYWHERE IN THE WORLD. KILLER WAVES CAN FORM IN DEEP LAKES. THEY CAN ALSO HAPPEN IN INLAND SEAS SUCH AS THE BALTIC SEA AND THE CASPIAN SEA. BUT MOST TSUNAMIS OCCUR IN THE PACIFIC OCEAN AND THE SEAS CONNECTED TO THE PACIFIC.

The Pacific is the world's largest ocean. It covers more than one-third of the Earth's surface. Millions of people who live along Pacific shores face the risk of a tsunami. The West Coast of the United States is particularly at risk. About 490 cities are close enough to the coast to be affected by a tsunami.

CANARY ISLAND VOLCANO

The Cumbre Vieja volcano is more than 2,400 km (1,500 miles) from the East Coast of the United States. It is in the Canary Islands. These islands are in the Atlantic Ocean south-west of Spain. However, some scientists think the volcano could send a tsunami 9 to 23 m high crashing over the East Coast of the United States. Part of the volcano broke loose and slipped towards the Atlantic Ocean during an eruption in 1949. Another eruption could make it tumble right into the ocean. The landslide could send monster waves heading towards the East Coast from the state of Maine to the state of Florida.

GROWING THREAT

Tsunamis cause the most damage along shores that are flat and not much higher than the ocean. Steep, hilly coasts act like walls that protect people from the full force of tsunamis. Many deaths in the 2004 Indian Ocean tsunami happened in places that were barely 1 m above sea level.

Damage from a tsunami usually is greatest close to the shore, but tsunamis can wash more than 300 m inland. They can also rush up rivers that empty into the ocean. During a 1960 tsunami in Hawaii, waves surged up the River Wailua and caused damage far from the ocean.

The number of people affected by tsunamis is rising. That's partly because more people are living along coasts where tsunamis may occur. In addition, human activity is increasing the risk of tsunami disasters. For example, wetlands lie along some coasts. Wetlands are covered by shallow water, trees, bushes and grass. The plants act as a barrier that protects the coast from tsunamis. Building houses and roads along the coasts sometimes destroys wetlands.

YEAR-ROUND DISASTERS

There is no tsunami season. Killer waves can form throughout the year. They can occur at any time of the day or night.

In the United States, only six disastrous tsunamis happened between 1945 and 2006. They killed more than 350 people and caused damage worth $500 million (about £250 million) in Alaska, Hawaii and along the West Coast. From 1900 to 2000, more than 140 damaging tsunamis took place throughout the world. They killed more than 70,000 people. However, even one tsunami can be a disaster. The Indian Ocean tsunami in 2004 killed more than 200,000 people – more than all the tsunamis of the 1900s.

BIG WAVES IN JAPAN

At least eight killer tsunamis have hit Japan during the last 400 years. The worst was in 1896, when waves almost 30 m high washed over the Sanriku area on the island of Honshu. They killed about 26,000 people. Sanriku was hit again in 1933. That year, waves 23 m high killed 3,000 people and sank 8,000 ships.

DISASTER ZONES

Tsunamis strike coasts around the world. This map shows just a few of the Earth's most severe tsunamis.

Japan
1896 (26,000 deaths)

Italy
1908 (200,000 deaths)

Japan
1933 (3,000 deaths)

EUROPE

ASIA

AFRICA

Asia and East Africa
2004 (200,000+ deaths)
Affected areas include
Indonesia, Sri Lanka, India,
Thailand, Maldives, Malaysia,
Myanmar, Bangladesh,
Somalia, Kenya, Tanzania
and the Seychelles.

AUSTRALIA

Indonesia
1883 (36,000 deaths)

Papua New Guinea
1998 (2,000+ deaths)

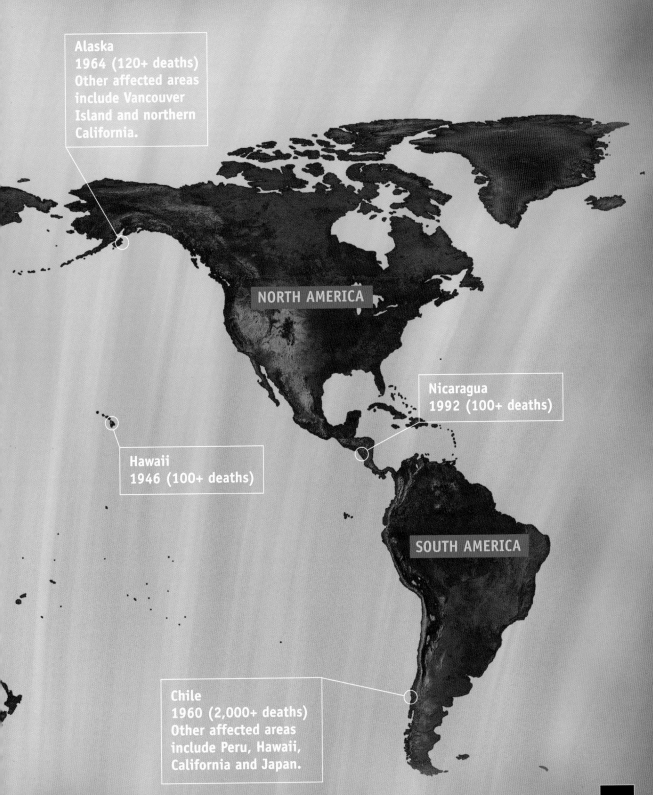

Alaska
1964 (120+ deaths)
Other affected areas
include Vancouver
Island and northern
California.

NORTH AMERICA

Nicaragua
1992 (100+ deaths)

Hawaii
1946 (100+ deaths)

SOUTH AMERICA

Chile
1960 (2,000+ deaths)
Other affected areas
include Peru, Hawaii,
California and Japan.

27 May, 1964
ALASKA

Valdez, Alaska, was seriously flooded after the 1964 tsunami.

When a tsunami struck in the spring of 1964, Doug McCrae was ready. He and his family knew about the danger of tsunamis. They lived in Seward, Alaska, USA. Earthquakes often cause tsunamis there. So when McCrae felt the shaking from one of Alaska's strongest earthquakes, he and his family got onto the roof of their house. *'We couldn't see it coming,'* McCrae said of the tsunami. *'But we could hear it coming.'* When the wall of water hit, it tore the house off the ground.

The tsunami took the family on a wild ride. As the house floated through the woods, McCrae worried that tree branches would scrape his family right off the roof. Finally, the house got stuck between some trees. The family escaped.

Hundreds of other people were not so lucky. The tsunami killed

about 120 from Alaska to California. A 9 m wave crashed down onto Valdez, Alaska. This town was right on the waterfront. People later rebuilt Valdez further from the water.

'It was like a jet landing on your roof.'

– Doug McCrae, describing the 1964 tsunami in Seward, Alaska

Charles Ford was taking a bath in his home almost 3,860 km (2,400 miles) away on Vancouver Island in Canada. He wondered why the bath took so long to drain. *'I went to the front door and found the water level at the top of the porch, which was about 3 feet [1 m] above the ground,'* he remembered. Water from the tsunami was rising up through the bathtub drainpipe.

People said the disaster was a 'tidal wave' from an earthquake in Alaska. *'Nothing happened for the next hour or so and we thought it was all over,'* Ford said, *'but then we heard the roar of rushing water.'* The water flooded his house, but he and his family escaped.

Soon people far to the south in Crescent City, California, were hearing the roar. The town of 7,500 people is right on the Pacific Ocean. The tsunami hit like a hammer. It flattened most of the city.

Gary Clawson's dad was having a birthday party in his family's restaurant when the 6 m wall of water arrived. It killed Clawson's dad, mum and his fiancée. *'You can't define how it felt, or what you go through when you can't breathe,'* Clawson said of his experience. *'You have to live [through it] to know what it's like.'*

27

Measuring Tsunamis

HOW DO YOU MEASURE A TSUNAMI? YOU CAN'T USE A RULER OR WEIGH IT ON A SCALE. ONE WAY IS TO MEASURE THE SIZE OF THE WAVES COMING ASHORE. A TSUNAMI WITH 6 M WAVES IS CERTAINLY STRONGER THAN A TSUNAMI WITH 30 CM WAVES.

Measuring the size and strength of a tsunami is important. It can give rescue workers an idea of how much damage the disaster may have caused. If a tsunami was very big and strong, rescue workers know they might need special tools and equipment to help people.

Scientists use tsunami measurements too. The information helps them to compare, study and understand tsunamis. They can learn, for instance, which earthquakes may cause tsunamis. Measurements also can help in working out how to make stronger buildings that don't fall apart in tsunamis.

APRIL FOOLS' TSUNAMI

It is 1 April 1946, a day like any other day. Vivian Aoki caught an early bus and arrived at her school in Laupahoehoe, Hawaii. But then a police officer came around. '[He] told the children to go to higher ground because a tsunami was coming,' Aoki remembered. The children didn't listen. They thought the police officer was playing a joke – after all, it was April Fools' Day. Other people had the same thought, before an earthquake in the Pacific Ocean set off a terrible tsunami. In Hawaii the 7 m waves killed more than 100 people, including students at Aoki's school.

A tsunami wave rumbles towards the shore of Hilo, Hawaii, in 1946, while a man watches from the pier *(arrow at left)*. This tsunami led to the establishment of a tsunami warning system.

TSUNAMI INTENSITY SCALES

A scientist named August Sieberg invented the first way of measuring tsunamis in 1927. Nicholas Ambraseys modified Sieberg's scale in 1962. The scale – which is no longer used by scientists – became known as the Sieberg-Ambraseys Tsunami Intensity Scale. It used six numbers to measure the amount of damage in a tsunami. However, it did not include enough numbers to give good measurements.

Through the years, other scientists have tried to invent better tsunami scales. They are still looking for a scale to measure tsunamis. Gerassimos Papadopoulos, of Greece, and Fumihiko Imamura, of Japan, invented one of the best scales in 2001. The 2001 tsunami scale measures tsunamis' effects on humans and property. It also measures the height of tsunami waves.

MEASURING THE DAMAGE

The 2001 tsunami scale considers a tsunami's effect on people and property. As a result, the waves in a tsunami measuring X on the scale may be no taller than the waves in a tsunami measuring IX. A tsunami that destroys people's homes will have a higher numeral than one that only slightly damages property – even if the tsunamis' waves were the same height.

SCALE OF DESTRUCTION

The 2001 tsunami scale uses the roman numerals I (one) to XII (twelve) to show the strength of a tsunami. A tsunami measuring I on the scale would be such a small wave that nobody would notice it. Only special instruments could tell that it happened. A tsunami measuring between II and IV on the scale would be noticeable, but it would not cause damage on the shore.

Gerassimos Papadopoulos

THE 2001 TSUNAMI SCALE

Papadopoulos and Imamura based their scale mainly on a tsunami's effects on people and property. They also included wave height estimates in their scale.

CATEGORY	STRENGTH/WAVE HEIGHT	EFFECT
I	NOT FELT	NONE
II	SCARCELY FELT	NONE
III	WEAK	MOST PEOPLE ON BOARD SMALL BOATS FEEL IT AND A FEW PEOPLE ON THE COAST SEE IT. NO DAMAGE OCCURS.
IV	LARGELY OBSERVED	PEOPLE ON BOARD LARGE AND SMALL SHIPS FEEL IT AND MOST PEOPLE ON THE COAST SEE IT. NO DAMAGE OCCURS.
V	STRONG (WAVES 1 M OR 3 FT HIGH)	A FEW PEOPLE ARE FRIGHTENED AND RUN TO HIGHER GROUND. MANY SMALL BOATS MOVE ONSHORE AND SOME CRASH INTO ONE ANOTHER OR OVERTURN. SOME FLOODING OF LAND ALONG THE SHORE OCCURS.
VI	SLIGHTLY DAMAGING (2 M OR 6 FT WAVES)	MANY PEOPLE ARE FRIGHTENED AND RUN TO HIGHER GROUND. MOST SMALL BOATS MOVE ONSHORE, CRASH INTO ONE ANOTHER OR OVERTURN. FLOODING AND DAMAGE TO A FEW WOODEN BUILDINGS OCCURS.
VII	DAMAGING (4 M OR 12 FT WAVES)	MANY PEOPLE ARE FRIGHTENED AND TRY TO RUN TO HIGHER GROUND. MANY SMALL BOATS ARE DAMAGED. MANY WOODEN BUILDINGS ARE DAMAGED AND SOME ARE SMASHED OR WASHED AWAY.
VIII	HEAVILY DAMAGING (4 M OR 12 FT WAVES)	A FEW PEOPLE ARE WASHED AWAY. MOST SMALL BOATS ARE DAMAGED AND MANY ARE WASHED AWAY. SOME LARGE BOATS MOVE ASHORE. A GREAT DEAL OF FLOODING OCCURS. MOST WOODEN BUILDINGS ARE SMASHED. SOME DAMAGE TO BRICK AND CONCRETE BUILDINGS OCCURS.
IX	DESTRUCTIVE (8 M OR 26 FT WAVES)	MANY PEOPLE ARE WASHED AWAY. MOST SMALL BOATS ARE DESTROYED OR WASHED AWAY. MANY LARGE BOATS MOVE FAR INSHORE AND SOME ARE DESTROYED. MORE DAMAGE TO BRICK AND CONCRETE BUILDINGS OCCURS.
X	VERY DESTRUCTIVE (8 M OR 26 FT WAVES)	PEOPLE EXPERIENCE PANIC AND MANY ARE WASHED AWAY. MOST LARGE BOATS MOVE ASHORE, AND MANY CARS OVERTURN AND FLOAT AWAY. MANY STRONG BRICK BUILDINGS ARE DAMAGED.
XI	DEVASTATING (16 M OR 52 FT WAVES)	LARGE FIRES OCCUR. CARS AND OTHER BIG OBJECTS ARE WASHED OUT TO SEA. BIG BOULDERS FROM THE SEA BOTTOM MOVE INLAND. WORSE DAMAGE TO BRICK AND CONCRETE BUILDINGS OCCURS.
XII	COMPLETELY DEVASTATING (32 M OR 104 FT WAVES)	ALMOST ALL BUILDINGS ARE DESTROYED OR DAMAGED.

A tsunami measuring V would have waves about 1 m high. It might cause a little flooding. A tsunami measuring VI or above is a different story. A tsunami such as this would have waves at least 2 m high. It would damage buildings and hurt people. A tsunami measuring VIII would have waves 4 m high. The waves could wash people out to sea, smash buildings and carry ships onto the land.

DEVASTATING TSUNAMIS

The worst tsunamis measure XI or XII. A tsunami measuring XI has waves 16 m high. These waves can sweep people away. They can carry cars into the ocean and cause other widespread damage.

A tsunami measuring XII is the worst. The scale calls these monsters 'completely devastating' tsunamis. Their waves are at least 32 m high and can even smash apart strong brick buildings.

Waves from the 1960 Chilean tsunami flooded the coast of Crescent City, California, USA.

The 2004 Indian Ocean tsunami swept this boat ashore in India.

The 2004 tsunami flooded this religious building in Sri Lanka.

1 September 1992
NICARAGUA

Only the foundation remains of a building after a tsunami struck Nicaragua, Central America, in 1992. Another building behind the ruined structure was mostly unharmed.

On 1 September 1992, Chris Terry and his friend Scott Willson were inside their fishing boat. It was floating near the town of San Juan del Sur in Nicaragua. There had been an earthquake earlier in the day under the Pacific Ocean. They had never even felt the earthquake, but they did notice something else quite odd.

'**We heard a slam,**' Terry remembered. They climbed up the stairs to the deck, where they could look outside. Their boat was sitting on the bottom of the harbour, which usually had water 6 m deep. A few seconds later, a huge wave tossed their boat around like a toy. Willson could see the lights from the village. '**And then the swell hit**', Terry said, '**and the lights went out, and we could hear people screaming.**'

People were screaming in twenty-seven towns and villages along 220 km (132 miles) of Nicaragua's Pacific

Coast. The earthquake had caused a tsunami. Its waves were up to 9 m high. Inez Ortega was making dinner in her restaurant along the beach. She noticed that the water seemed kind of low. When she glanced outside again, a giant wall of water was rushing over the beach towards the restaurant.

'*I started running,*' she remembered, '*but I didn't even get out of the restaurant when the wave hit.*' The tsunami turned the restaurant into a swimming pool filled with broken chairs and floating tables. It took her half an hour to swim out.

The tsunami killed more than one hundred people and injured many others. Some drowned, and others were badly hurt when the waves threw them against the ground. The waves picked up cars and lorries and smashed them into houses. It destroyed the homes of 13,000 people.

Many other people also felt the tsunami's effects. Thousands of people along Nicaragua's coast were fishermen or worked in factories that prepared fish for market. The tsunami destroyed most of Nicaragua's Pacific Ocean fishing boats. People had no jobs for months until fishermen could buy new boats.

Scientists later discovered that this was a very unusual earthquake called a tsunami earthquake. It was quite strong, measuring 7.6 on the Richter scale. The earthquake's shock waves did not cause a lot of ground shaking. The shaking might have warned people that a tsunami could happen. Instead, the quake's force stayed under the ocean and produced a tsunami. Only about 10 out of every 100 earthquakes that cause tsunamis are this very dangerous kind.

Debris littered a beach in Nicaragua following the 1992 tsunami.

'Suddenly the boat whipped around very, very fast.'

– Chris Terry, who was at sea off the coast of Nicaragua during a 1992 tsunami

People Helping People

WHEN THE WATER PULLED BACK AFTER THE 2004 INDIAN OCEAN TSUNAMI, IT LEFT A TRAIL OF DESTRUCTION. MORE THAN 500,000 PEOPLE IN SOUTHERN ASIA AND EASTERN AFRICA HAD BROKEN BONES, CUTS AND OTHER INJURIES. THEY NEEDED DOCTORS AND NURSES, BUT THE MONSTER WAVES HAD SMASHED HOSPITALS AND DOCTORS' OFFICES. ALSO MANY DOCTORS AND NURSES HAD DIED OR BEEN SERIOUSLY INJURED.

About one million people had nowhere to live. The tsunami had washed away their homes. Shops were washed away too. People couldn't buy food or bottled water. They didn't have basic supplies. Soap? Toothpaste? Warm blankets? None of these things were available.

Some people had no clothing at all. The rushing water had torn it right off their bodies. The tsunami knocked down power lines. Telephones were dead. The waves flooded and destroyed cars and lorries. They wouldn't have been much use because roads and bridges had been washed away.

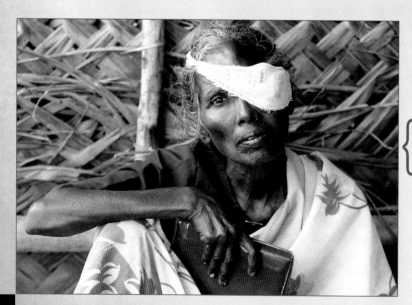

An Indian woman injured by the 2004 tsunami rests in her new house.

36

Residents of a Sri Lankan village examine a bridge that was destroyed by the 2004 Indian Ocean tsunami.

NEIGHBOURS HELPING NEIGHBOURS

Survivors of a disaster often experience stress. They just had a terrifying experience. They saw horrible things happen all around them. 'I saw a dead boy, aged about four, being carried away by his father,' said Joni Makivirta, who was in Thailand after the 2004 tsunami. 'It was terrible.' Ranil Ariyarathna, who was in Sri Lanka, remembered, 'All I could hear was screaming. Then everyone vanished in a second when out of nowhere a wave appeared.'

Everything may seem hopeless after a disaster, but help and hope soon began to arrive. The first help usually comes from people nearby. They can reach the disaster scene fast. By helping to rescue victims trapped under wreckage and treating injured people, they can keep a disaster from getting worse.

GOLDEN 72 HOURS

Immediate help is so important that the first three days after a disaster are called the golden 72 hours. They are a golden opportunity to save the lives of people who are trapped or hurt. Fast action also can keep healthy survivors from getting sick.

People with broken bones, bad cuts and other injuries need medical care. Without it, they may get worse or die. Disasters often leave people trapped under broken buildings. If not rescued quickly, they may die – especially if they are badly hurt.

All the survivors need water to drink. There may be lots of water on the ground after a tsunami, but it is often dirty. Germs in the water can make people sick. Survivors need clean water. They also need warm clothing, shelter from the weather and food.

Soldiers unload drinking water and other relief items to distribute to Indian victims of the 2004 tsunami.

Refugees in Indonesia pass body bags lying on the ground after the 2004 Indian Ocean tsunami.

DISASTER RELIEF WORKERS

Large scale disasters are rare in the United Kingdom, when they do happen the first help usually comes from the fire service and the police. They arrive at the disaster scene quickly. If the disaster is serious, soldiers from the British army will be called in to help. Disaster relief will be organized by the Emergency Planning Officers from government departments. Workers from other organizations such as the Red Cross, the St John Ambulance service and the Salvation Army may also arrive. Help from other nations is important after a disaster – especially when disasters strike developing countries. Damage was enormous in many countries hit by the Indian Ocean tsunami. These countries did not have enough money to recover by themselves.

This village near the coast of Sumatra was almost entirely wiped out by the 2004 tsunami.

'It's totally destroyed,' said Chris Rainier of Banda Aceh, Indonesia, after the Indian Ocean tsunami. 'The buildings have been flattened . . . and entire communities, probably something like a hundred thousand people, have been swept out to sea.'

MANY HELPING HANDS

In developing countries, help often comes from the International Federation of Red Cross and Red Crescent Societies. This is the world's biggest private organization that helps in disasters. Red Cross and Red Crescent workers stay for months or years to help people rebuild their lives.

Nearly every country has a Red Cross or Red Crescent organization. When a disaster strikes, people in each country can help by sending money to those, or other organizations. In the UK the Disasters Emergency Committee raised £390 million to help people whose lives had been destroyed by the Indian Ocean tsunami.

TSUNAMI
EMERGENCY HEALTH SER

MOBILE HEALTH PROGRA
POOMPUHAR

RLHP-SNEHA

Sponsored by:-TdH (Ger

Many relief organizations flocked to southern Asia after the 2004 tsunami. These organizations provided medicine *(above)*, food, shelter and clothing.

There are many other helping hands. The United Nations, a group of more than 190 countries, provides a lot of disaster relief. Governments of other countries send workers and money. Private businesses also help.

The Malaysian navy loaded a ship with medical items to deliver to Indonesia after the 2004 tsunami.

RELIEF AND RECOVERY

The first help for survivors often comes in special kits that relief workers hand out. These packages contain water, food, blankets, tents and other things people need to stay healthy until more help arrives.

After the Indian Ocean tsunami, UNICEF (the United Nations Children's Fund) delivered thousands of kits to help children and their families. 'We've provided these families with the things they tell us [they] need the most,' said UNICEF health worker Myo Tint. 'Clothes and blankets to keep children warm and basic household items they can't easily replace.'

After relief comes recovery, in which people rebuild homes, communities and lives. Recovery may take years when a disaster causes damage in a big area. Experts think it may take ten years for Indian Ocean countries to recover from the great tsunami of 2004.

THE FIRE TSUNAMI

Eyewitnesses said that water in a 1998 Papua New Guinea tsunami glowed as it crashed down, as if it were on fire. The bodies of some victims looked like they had been burned. People said it was a 'fire tsunami'. Later, however, scientists solved the mystery. The water glowed because it was full of dinoflagellates – tiny creatures that glow like fireflies. The burns? Water in the tsunami was filled with sand and it scraped away victims' skin and made it look burned.

Many Thais had to live in tents after the
2004 tsunami destroyed their homes.

SPRINGING BACK

Even in the most terrible disasters, people do spring back. They rebuild homes, schools, roads and cities. Most important of all, they get their own lives back.

Till Mayer, a journalist working for the Red Cross, saw clean-up efforts begin after the 2004 Indian Ocean tsunami. He was in Sri Lanka, one of the countries where there was great damage. 'There is not only destruction to see,' he said. 'Everywhere along the coasts of Sri Lanka people are still clearing up and sometimes even beginning to rebuild. . . . From the debris the tsunami victims collect what is useful for reconstruction: roofing tiles [and] stones.'

Indonesians worked with elephants to clear debris left by the 2004 tsunami.

Survivors of the 2004 tsunami, like these people in India, continue to work hard to rebuild their villages.

'I realize that we will need a long time to recover from the tsunami. But the spirit and determination of the people will help us not only to rebuild Aceh but to make it even a better place than it used to be before.'

– Saifullah Akbar, a relief organization supervisor who is helping to rebuild in Banda Aceh, Indonesia, after the 2004 Indian Ocean tsunami

17 July, 1998
PAPUA NEW GUINEA

Only rubble remained of a school in Sissano, Papua New Guinea, after the 1998 tsunami.

It was a pleasant Friday evening in 1998. Children were playing on the beach just before sunset. They were looking forward to parties that started a four-day holiday in Papua New Guinea, an island nation in the west Pacific Ocean. Adults were walking along the beach and visiting friends and relatives. Suddenly, big cracks opened in the sand. The children called for the adults to come and see.

An earthquake had cracked the ground. People crowded the beach to take a look. Their eyes soon shifted to the ocean, where something very strange was happening. The water was rushing away from the shore, as if sucked up by a giant straw.

People in other villages saw the same sight. Then they heard a roar. Some thought an aeroplane was flying overhead. But the roar was the ocean. It was coming back in a wall of foaming water. In some places, the wall was more than 9 m high. Water that high would reach the third-floor windows on a building. '*We just saw the sea rise up and it came towards the village and we had to run for our lives,*' said Paul Saroya, who was in one village.

The wall of water crashed onto the shore. It rushed into the villages. It drowned people, including eight members of Saroya's family. It completely swept away three villages where more than 7,000 people lived.

People had almost no warning that a killer wave was on the way. Only a few minutes passed between the earthquake and the tsunami. There was no time to get away from the shore.

'*I felt the earthquake rocking the house,*' said Raymond Nimis. '*Then we heard the sea break. I saw it, very huge, we tried to run but it was too late. The wave crashed onto the house. People were dying everywhere, some died under the house, others got rolled in by the wave.*' One of those who died was Nimis's one-year-old daughter.

Austen Crapp ran a health clinic in Arop, a village where 1,800 people lived. '*There is nothing left of that place except clean sand,*' he said. '*When the wave hit, that was the end of it.*'

As the water flowed back, it carried hundreds of people out to sea, where they died. A few minutes later, a second big wall of water rushed in and then a third.

The tsunamis from that same earthquake washed over other villages in Papua New Guinea. More than 2,000 people were killed, and hundreds of others were injured.

Many people were injured by the 1998 tsunami.

47

The Future

We learn lessons from past disasters. These lessons can make life safer for people in the future. The 2004 Indian Ocean tsunami, for instance, made people realize that the world needed better tsunami warning systems. Many of those who died in the disaster had no warning at all.

It took hours for the waves to travel across the ocean. Had a warning gone out, people could have escaped the waves just by getting off the beach. Those working in nearby hotels, restaurants and shops also could have evacuated (left for a safer area). Instead, they stayed, and many died.

BETTER TSUNAMI ALARMS

In the future, more people will get a warning before the waves hit. The Indian Ocean tsunami got the attention of governments all around the world. It made leaders more aware of the death and damage that tsunamis can cause.

WAVE UPON WAVE

Many people die in tsunamis because they don't know that tsunamis are not just one big wave. The waves may be more than thirty minutes apart. The first wave often is not the biggest. After the first wave, people may gather on the shore to see the damage. Then another wave may rush in and kill them. It is much safer to leave the area and stay away.

Villagers and tourists fled from a tsunami wave that crashed ashore at Koh Raya, Thailand, in 2004.

Governments are building new tsunami warning systems. The new systems will work better and have fewer false alarms. From 1948 to 2000, about 75 per cent of tsunami warnings were false alarms. False alarms are bad. If officials predict a tsunami and nothing happens, people may ignore the next warning – and get caught in a real tsunami. The false warnings also may make thousands of people flee an area very quickly. People may be hurt or killed while evacuating. False alarms are expensive too. They make people lose time from work and school.

TONNES OF TSUNAMETERS

In the past, scientists sent out tsunami alerts after a certain kind of strong undersea earthquake occurred. But there was no way to tell whether the quake really would cause a tsunami. In the future, scientists will be able to tell.

New tools called tsunameters allow scientists to predict tsunamis. Tsunameters stand guard in the world's oceans. These electronic devices can detect tsunami waves passing through the ocean water. People on boats usually cannot see the waves of a tsunami passing underneath them, but tsunameters can detect them under the water.

One part of the tsunameter sits right on the ocean floor. When a wave sweeps over a tsunameter, it signals a nearby buoy. The buoy is a package of instruments that floats on the water's surface. The buoy sends the alarm to a satellite (an unmanned spacecraft) orbiting the Earth. Finally, the satellite uses a radio signal to pass the alert to scientists and emergency workers.

A 1964 tsunami in Alaska flooded this village and destroyed homes.

A tsunameter buoy floats in the Pacific Ocean. You can see readings from tsunameters in the Deep Ocean Assessment and Reporting of Tsunamis (DART) programme on the Internet (www.ndbc.noaa.gov/dart.shtml).

THROWING DARTS

A few tsunameters already stood guard over the Pacific Ocean in 2004. These tsunameters were part of the Deep Ocean Assessment and Reporting of Tsunamis programme. The US agency NOAA (National Oceanic and Atmospheric Administration) was in charge of this programme.

After the Indian Ocean tsunami, NOAA decided to add about thirty tsunameters to DART. They will give more accurate tsunami warnings for people on the West Coast of the United States. In addition, they will help protect other countries along the Pacific Ocean. In the future, tsunameters also may protect people along the Atlantic coasts too.

Warning systems such as DART may protect other oceans as well. After the 2004 tsunami, many countries started thinking about creating their own warning systems. India, for instance, said it might put tsunameters in the Indian Ocean.

WHEN THE OCEAN SAYS 'RUN!'

The first sign of a tsunami often comes from the ocean. Just before a tsunami crashes down, water may rush back into the ocean. People can see the ocean floor far beyond what's visible at low tide. They may even see fish flopping on the sand. When the water goes away like that, it soon may be heading back in a huge wave.

SMARTER COMPUTERS

Computers are an important part of tsunami warning systems. Readings from tsunameters go into computers, which help scientists decide whether a tsunami is possible. In the future, those computers will be faster and more powerful. They will also have better programs. As scientists learn more about tsunamis, they write programs that make better predictions. People have known about tsunamis for more than 2,400 years. Until the Indian Ocean tsunami, however, scientists paid very little attention to these disasters.

Scientists run a computer simulation of a
tsunami. Scientists use this information to
learn more about tsunamis.

EDUCATION SAVES LIVES

While better tsunami warning systems are important, warnings alone are not enough to save lives. People must know what to do when they get tsunami warnings. There may not be much time. So people must act fast.

The most important action is to get away from the ocean. Move inland to higher ground. If the land is flat all around or if there is not enough time to get away, go to the upper floor of a nearby building. Stay there until you are sure it is safe to leave.

Tsunamis are frightening and dangerous, but they are also rare. Don't let the risk of a tsunami spoil your fun at the beach. Better tsunami warnings and information on tsunami safety can protect most people from these monster waves.

TSUNAMI SAFETY

You and your family can follow these basic tips to stay safe in a tsunami emergency.

- Pay attention to tsunami warnings on TV or the radio. Follow all emergency instructions.

- If you are at the beach or by the ocean during an earthquake, move inland right away. In areas near the water, an earthquake can be a natural tsunami warning.

- Water that suddenly rushes away from the beach is another natural tsunami warning. You may see rocks, shells and flopping fish where the water disappeared. Don't stand there and look. The water may rush back in and sweep you away.

- If there is no time to get away from the ocean in a tsunami warning, go to the upper floor of a hotel or other tall, strong building. If no buildings are nearby, look for trees or other objects that you can climb to get above the waves.

- Remember that a tsunami is one wave after another. Don't go near the shore after the first or second wave. Another wave may be coming.

- Water in a tsunami may pick up bacteria as it washes over the land. These germs could make you very sick. Don't play in the water.

- If you are swept up in a tsunami, try to stay as calm as possible. Keep your head above the water. Watch for tree branches, telephone poles or other objects that you can grab and hold to stay afloat.

Timeline

AD 365 The Thera volcano erupts, causing a tsunami that strikes the Greek island of Crete. The waves also reach Alexandria, Egypt, striking with such force that they carry ships inland.

1703 The Genroku Kanto earthquake causes a tsunami that hits the coastal area of Japan, killing thousands of people.

1746 A large earthquake in central Peru causes a tsunami that destroys the town of Callao. Eyewitnesses say the first wave was 24 m high.

1755 An earthquake in Lisbon, Portugal, causes many citizens to seek safety on ships in the port – and then a tsunami demolishes the port *(right)*. About 100,000 people in Portugal, Morocco and Spain are killed.

1771 A tsunami hits the Ryukyu Islands in Japan, killing more than 13,000 people.

1868 The US warship USS *Wateree* is carried about 457 m inland when a tsunami follows an 8.5 earthquake in Arica, Chile *(left)*.

1883 About 36,000 people die from the tsunami that followed the eruption of Krakatau in Indonesia.

1896 Citizens gather to celebrate a religious festival in Sanriku, Japan, when a tsunami strikes and claims approximately 26,000 lives.

1908 A 7.5-magnitude quake in southern Italy causes a tsunami that claims up to 200,000 lives.

1923 The Great Kanto earthquake in Japan, combined with fires and tsunamis, kills 140,000 people.

1927 August Sieberg invents the first scale for measuring tsunamis.

1933 Tsunami waves reaching 23 m in height strike Sanriku, killing 3,000 people and sinking 8,000 ships.

1946 An earthquake in the Aleutian Islands in Alaska destroys the Scotch Cap Lighthouse. Five hours later, a tsunami strikes Hilo, Hawaii.

1958 A magnitude 8 earthquake causes a landslide in Lituya Bay, Alaska. The landslide then produces a tsunami.

1960 A 9.5-magnitude earthquake causes a tsunami in Chile *(right)*. The tsunami waves travel to Hilo, Hawaii and Japan.

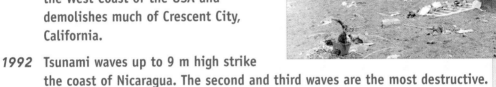

1964 An earthquake in Anchorage, Alaska, causes a landslide. The landslide then causes a tsunami that sweeps down to the West Coast of the USA and demolishes much of Crescent City, California.

1992 Tsunami waves up to 9 m high strike the coast of Nicaragua. The second and third waves are the most destructive.

1998 A tsunami strikes Papua New Guinea, killing more than 2,000 people and leaving thousands homeless.

2001 Gerassimos Papadopoulos and Fumihiko Imamura invent a more accurate scale for measuring tsunamis.

2004 A tsunami in the Indian Ocean kills more than 200,000 people in southern Asia, South-east Asia and eastern Africa.

2005 A tsunami follows an 8.7-magnitude earthquake in western Sumatra *(left)*. The disasters displaced 140,000 people.

Glossary

asteroid: a piece of rock in outer space

comet: a large piece of ice and dust in outer space

earthquake: a shaking of the ground caused by forces below the Earth's surface

evacuate: to leave a dangerous area and go somewhere safe

Krakatau: a volcano in Indonesia that exploded and caused one of the world's worst tsunamis in 1883

landslide: the fast, downward movement of earth or rock

Richter scale: a scale used for measuring earthquakes

satellite: a small, unmanned spacecraft that circles high above the Earth's surface

Sieberg-Ambraseys Tsunami Intensity Scale: a scale for measuring tsunamis. The scale used six numbers for measuring the amount of damage a tsunami caused. August Sieberg developed the scale in 1927, and Nicholas Ambraseys modified it in 1962.

tidal wave: a wave produced by the daily rising and falling of ocean waters

tsunameter: an electronic device that can detect tsunami waves passing through the ocean water

tsunami: a wave produced by earth movement, a volcano or a landslide

volcano: a hole in the Earth's crust that can erupt giving out hot rock and steam

wetland: a vegetation-rich area that lies along some coasts. Wetlands are natural barriers that help protect the land from the effects of tsunamis.

Places to Visit

The Science Museum, London, UK
www.sciencemuseum.org.uk
The Science Museum in London has a video exhibition called the 'Forces of Nature2D'. This short film showcases the awesome spectacle of earthquakes, volcanoes, tsunamis and severe storms.

Source Notes

4 Rick Von Feldt, 'Nature's Ugly Hand: What We Saw,' *Tsunami Survivor Stories*, 1 January 2005, http://phukettsunami.blogspot.com/2005/01/natures-ugly-hand-what-we-saw.html (15 September 2005).

4 Simon Clark, quoted in 'Eyewitnesses Recount Tsunami Terror,' *CNN.com*, June 23 2005, http://www.cnn.com/2004/WORLD/asiapcf/12/26/asia.quake.eyewitness (15 September 2005).

5 Boree Carlsson, quoted in 'Eyewitnesses Recount Tsunami Terror,' *CNN.com*, 23 June 2005, http://www.cnn.com/2004/WORLD/asiapcf/12/26/asia.quake.eyewitness (15 September 2005).

5 Les Boardman, quoted in Alan Morison, 'Survivor's Tale: This Is Surreal,' *CNN.com*, June 23 2005, http://edition.cnn.com/2004/WORLD/asiapcf/12/26/asia.quake.moro/ (5 November 2005).

5 Boree Carlsson.

10 Sonam Kalra, quoted in 'Tsunami Tragedy: Your E-mails,' *CNN.com*, January 24 2005, http://www.cnn.com/2004/WORLD/asiapcf/12/28/more.emails/ (15 September 2005).

11 Howard Ulrich, quoted in 'July 10, 1958 Southeastern Alaska Tsunami – Lituya Bay Narrative,' NOAA National Weather Service,' n.d., http://wcatwc.arh.noaa.gov/web_tsus/19580710/narrative1.htm (1 February 2006).

12–13 'The Explosion of Krakatoa Mountain,' *Intisari* (August 1982), quoted in *The Indonesian Digest*, n.d., http://www.indodigest.com/indonesia-special-article-16.html (16 September 2005).

13 Ibid.

21 Susan Maeda Veriato, quoted in *Pacific Tsunami Museum Homepage*, n.d., http://www.tsunami.org (6 September 2005).

21 Ibid.

21 James Fujimoto, quoted in Lori Kawamura, 'What a Morning!!,' *Pacific Tsunami Museum*, n.d., http://www.tsunami.org/essay99b.htm (September 6 2005).

26 Doug McCrae, quoted in Yereth Rosen, 'Tsunami Experience Prepares Alaska Town for Next One,' *Reuters News Service*, 1 June 2005, http://www.planetark.com/avantgo/dailynewsstory.cfm?newsid=28822 (30 August 2005).

27 Charles Ford, 'Tidal Wave,' *Times Colonist*, (Victoria, BC), quoted in *Provincial Emergency Program*, n.d., http://www.pep.bc.ca/hazard_preparedness/zeballos_64/tidalwave.html (27 August 2005).

27 Gary Clawson, quoted in Willie Drye, 'California Tsunami Victims Recall 1964's Killer Waves,' *National Geographic News*, 21 January 2005, http://news.nationalgeographic.com/news/2005/01/0121

_050121_1964_tsunami.html (27 August 2005).

27 Doug McCrae.

28 Vivian Aoki, quoted in Wesley Ching, 'April Fool's Disaster,' *Pacific Tsunami Museum*, n.d., http://www|.tsunami.org/essay98c.htm (6 September 2005).

34 Chris Terry, quoted in Tim Folger, 'Waves of Destruction,' *Discover*, 5 January 2005, http://www.discover.com/web-exclusives/waves-of-destruction (7, September 2005).

35 Inez Ortega, quoted in Tim Folger, 'Waves of Destruction,' *Discover*, 5 January 2005, http://www.discover.com/web-exclusives/waves-of-destruction (7 September 2005).

35 Chris Terry.

38 Joni Makivirta, quoted in 'Tsunami Tragedy: Your E-mails,' *CNN.com*, January 24 2005, http://www.cnn.com/2004/WORLD/asiapcf/12/28/more.emails/ (15 September 2005).

38 Ranil Ariyarathna, quoted in 'Tsunami Tragedy: Your E-mails,' *CNN.com*, 24 January 2005, http://www.cnn.com/2004/WORLD/asiapcf/12/28/more.emails/ (15 September 2005).

40 Chris Rainier and David Braun, 'Tsunami Eyewitness Account by Nat Geo Photographer,' *National Geographic*, 11 January 2005, http://news.nationalgeographic.com/news/2005/01/0111_050111_tsunami_sumatra.html (15 September 2005).

42 Myo Tint, quoted in 'Helping Families Get Back on Their Feet in Myanmar,' *UNICEF*, 14 January 2005, http://www.unicef.org/myanmar/health_nutrition_1612.html (16 September 2005).

44 Till Mayer, 'Reconstruction and Invisible Scars,' *CNN.com*, 26 January 2005, http://www.cnn.com/2005/WORLD/asiapcf/01/02/srilanka.redcross/ (September 15 2005).

45 Saifullah Akbar, quoted in Mona Laczo, 'Steps to Rebuilding Aceh,' *Oxfam GB*, 2006, http://www.oxfam.org.uk/what_we_do/emergencies/country/asiaquake/reports/rebuildaceh_mona.htm (March 22 2006).

47 Colin Travertz, quoted in 'Thousands Missing after Papua New Guinea Tidal Waves,' *CNN.com*, July 21, 1998, http://www.cnn.com/WORLD/asiapcf/9807/21/papua.aftermath.01/ (December 9 2005).

47 Paul Saroya, quoted in 'The Earthquake and Tsunami of 17 July 1998 in Papua-New Guinea (PNG),' *The Tsunami Page of Dr. George P.C.*, n.d., http://www.drgeorgepc.com/Tsunami1998PNG.html (August 27 2005).

47 Raymond Nimis, quoted in 'Thousands Missing after Papua New Guinea Tidal Waves,' *CNN.com*, July 21, 1998, http://www.cnn.com/WORLD/asiapcf/9807/21/papua.aftermath.01/ (November 5 2005).

47 Austen Crapp, quoted in 'At Least 71 Killed in Papua New Guinea Tidal Wave,' *CNN.com*, July 18, 1998, http://www.cnn.com/WORLD/asiapcf/9807/18/tidal.wave.02 (August 27 2005).

Selected Bibliography

Dudley, Walter, and Min Lee. *Tsunami*. Honolulu: University of Hawai'i Press, 1998.

Engelbert, Phillis. *Dangerous Planet: The Science of Natural Disasters*. Detroit: UXL, 2001.

Gregory, Kenneth John, ed. *The Earth's Natural Forces*. New York: Oxford University Press, 1990.

Hancock, Paul L., and Brian J. Skinner. *Oxford Companion to the Earth*. Oxford, NY: Oxford University Press, 2000.

Powers, Dennis M. *The Raging Sea: The Powerful Account of the Worst Tsunami in U.S. History*. New York: Kensington Publishing, 2005.

Prager, Ellen J. *Furious Earth: The Science and Nature of Earthquakes, Volcanoes, and Tsunamis*. New York: McGraw-Hill, 2000.

Robinson, Andrew. *Earth Shock*. New York: W. W. Norton, 1993.

Spignesi, Stephen J. *The 100 Greatest Disasters of All Time*. New York: Kensington Publishing Corp., 2002.

Zebrowski, Ernest, Jr. *Perils of a Restless Planet: Scientific Perspectives on Natural Disasters*. New York: Cambridge University Press, 1997.

Zeilinga de Boer, Jelle, and Donald Theodore Sanders. *Earthquakes in Human History: The Far-Reaching Effects of Seismic Disruptions*. Princeton: Princeton University Press, 2005.

Further Resources

BOOKS

Baldwin, Carol. *Wild Water - Floods* (Raintree Freestyle: Turbulent Planet) Raintree Publishers, 2005.

Barber, Nicola. *Floods* (Our Violent Earth) Hodder Wayland, 2005.

Carruthers, Margaret W. *Tsunamis* (Watts Library: Earth Science) Franklin Watts, 2005.

Claybourne, Anna. *Extreme Earth* (100 Things You Should Know About) Miles Kelly Publishing Ltd, 2006.

Langley, Andrew. *Hurricanes. Tsunamis and Other Natural Disasters* (Kingfisher Knowledge) Kingfisher, 2006.

Langley, Andrew. *Natural Disasters* (Kingfisher Knowledge) Kingfisher, 2006.

Rooney, Anne. *Tsunami!* (Nature's Fury) Franklin Watts Ltd, 2006.

Spilsbury, Louise and Richard Spilsbury. *Sweeping Tsunamis* (Awesome Forces of Nature) Heinemann Library, 2005.

Spilsbury, Richard and Louise Spilsbury. *Tsunamis* (Natural Disasters) Hodder Wayland, 2007.

Steele, Chris. *Tsunamis* (Nature on the Rampage) Raintree, 2004.

Townsend, John. *The Asian Tsunami 2004* (When Disaster Struck) Raintree Publishers, 2007.

Townsend, John. *Tsunami Diary* (Livewire Non Fiction) Hodder Murray, 2006.

Violent Planet (Phenomena) Ticktock Media Ltd, 2006.

Watts, Claire. *Natural Disasters: Discover the Awesome Power of Tsunamis, Hurricanes, Earthquakes and Volcanoes* (Eyewitness Guide) Dorling Kindersley Publishers Ltd, 2006.

WEBSITES AND FILMS

The Disaster Area

http://www.fema.gov/kids/dizarea.htm
It's important to learn how to survive a natural disaster. This site provides fun ways to learn about keeping safe.

Killer Wave! Tsunami

http://www.nationalgeographic.com/ngkids/9610/kwave
This National Geographic site gives information about tsunamis and includes a survival story from the Hilo, Hawaii, tsunami of 1946.

Tsunami Activities

http://www.enchantedlearning.com/subjects/tsunami/activities.shtml
Visit this site for tsunami information, activities, and printouts.

Tsunami: The Big Wave

http://observe.arc.nasa.gov/nasa/exhibits/tsunami/tsun_bay.html
This slide show presentation provides a wide range of information about tsunamis.

Tsunami: Killer Wave. Washington, DC: National Geographic Society, 1997.

Tsunami 2004: Waves of Death. DVD. New York: History Channel, 2005.

Tsunami - The Killer Wave. DVD. London: BBC, 2005

Index

Photo Acknowledgements

The images in this book are used with the permission of: Courtesy of the National Oceanic and Atmospheric Administration Central Library Photo Collection, pp. 1, 8 (top), 11, 17, 20, 26, 27, 29, 31, 50, 51, 55; Courtesy National Information Service for Earthquake Engineering, University of California, Berkeley, pp. 3, 9, 19, 56 (both); © Reuters/CORBIS, p. 4; © Taiwan National Space Program Office/Handout/Reuters/CORBIS, p. 5; © Ron Dahlquist/SuperStock, p. 6; © Wilfried Strauch, pp. 7, 34, 35; AP Photo/Vincent Thian, p. 8 (bottom); © LANA SLIVAR/Reuters/CORBIS, p. 10; © CORBIS, p. 12; © North Wind Picture Archives, p. 13; © Pacific Tsunami Museum , pp. 16, 21 (top), 57 (top); AP Photo/Gemunu Amarasinghe, p. 18; © Earthquake Research Institute, University of Tokyo/USGS Circular 1187, p. 21 (bottom); Courtesy of Gerassimos Papadopoulos, p. 30; AP Photo/Jasper Juinen, pp. 32 (bottom), 36, 45; Wallace Griffin/USGS Circular 1187, p. 32 (top); © THOMAS WHITE/Reuters/CORBIS, p. 33; AP Photo/Eranga Jayawardena, p. 37; AP Photo/Manish Swarup, p. 38; © ADEK BERRY/AFP/Getty Images, p. 39; © Philip A. McDaniel/US Navy/ZUMA Press, p. 40; © Joerg Boethling/GlobalAware.org, p. 41; AP Photo/Teh Eng Koon, p. 42; AP Photo/Vincent Yu, p. 43; © TARMIZY HARVA/Reuters/CORBIS, p. 44; © Brian Cassey, p. 46; AP Photo/Brian Cassey, p. 47; © Photodisc/Getty Images, p. 48; © John Russell/AFP/Getty Images, p. 49; © Carlos Munoz-Yague/Eurelios/Photo Researchers, Inc., p. 53; © KIMIMASA MAYAMA/Reuters/CORBIS, p. 57 (bottom). Diagram by © Bill Hauser/Independent Picture Service, p. 15.

Front cover: AP Photo/APTN; Back cover: Courtesy of the National Oceanic and Atmospheric Administration Central Library Photo Collection.

This book was first published in the United States of America in 2007.

Copyright © 2007 by Michael Woods and Mary B Woods

About the Authors

Michael Woods is a science and medical journalist in Washington, D.C., who has won many national writing awards. He works in the Washington Bureau of the *Pittsburgh Post-Gazette* and the *Toledo Blade*. Mary B Woods has been a librarian in the Fairfax County Public School System in Virginia and the Benjamin Franklin International School in Barcelona, Spain. Their past books include the eight-volume Ancient Technology series. Michael and Mary have four children. When not writing, reading, or enjoying their grandchildren, Michael and Mary travel to gather material for future books.